How to use your Snap Revision \

This 'A Christmas Carol' Snap Workbook will help you t
mark in your AQA English Literature exam. Questions a
grouped into plot; setting and context; characters; themes; and exam
practice, and are designed to help you fully prepare for the exam.

Revise 1, 2 and 3
Short tasks progressing in level as you work through the topic.

Extend
Longer, essay-style questions to be completed on separate pieces of paper.

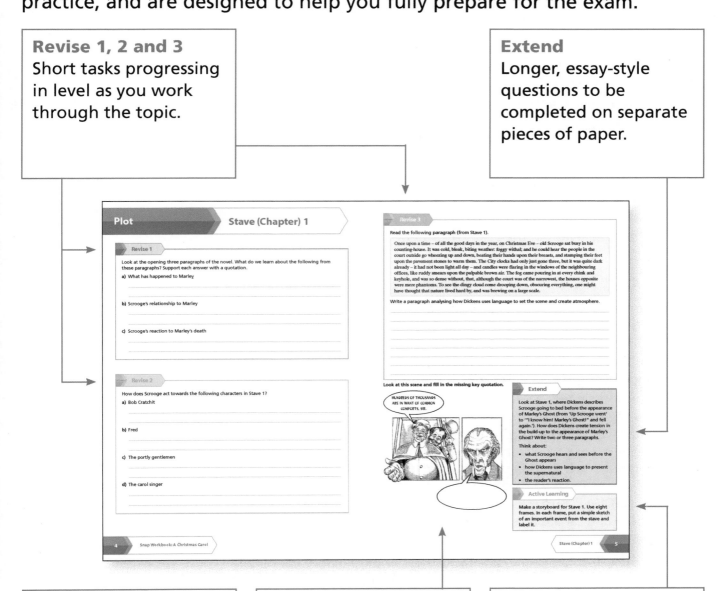

Answers
Provided at the back of the book.

Comic strips
Show key scenes from the text and include blank speech bubbles for you to fill in the missing key quotations from memory.

Active learning
Interactive tasks such as creating posters, storyboards and newspaper articles.

AUTHOR: PAUL BURNS

Published by Collins
An imprint of HarperCollins*Publishers*
1 London Bridge Street
London SE1 9GF

HarperCollins*Publishers*
1st Floor, Watermarque Building,
Ringsend Road, Dublin 4, Ireland

ISBN 9780008355289

First published 2019

10 9 8 7 6 5

British Library Cataloguing in Publication Data.

A CIP record of this book is available from the British Library.

Commissioning Editor: Clare Souza
Managing Editor: Shelley Teasdale
Author: Paul Burns
Copyeditor and project management: Fiona Watson
Typesetting: Jouve India Private Limited
Cover designers: Kneath Associates and Sarah Duxbury
Inside concept design: Ian Wrigley
Illustrations: Rose and Thorn Creative Services Ltd
Production: Karen Nulty
Printed and bound in the UK using 100% Renewable Electricity at CPI Group (UK) Ltd

ACKNOWLEDGEMENTS

The author and publisher are grateful to the copyright holders for permission to use quoted materials and images.

Every effort has been made to trace copyright holders and obtain their permission for the use of copyright material. The author and publisher will gladly receive information enabling them to rectify any error or omission in subsequent editions. All facts are correct at time of going to press.

MIX
Paper from
responsible source
FSC™ C007454

This book is produced from independently certified FSC™ paper to ensure responsible forest management.

For more information visit:
www.harpercollins.co.uk/green

Contents

Revise 1

Look at the opening three paragraphs of the novel. What do we learn about the following from these paragraphs? Support each answer with a quotation.

a) What has happened to Marley

....

....

b) Scrooge's relationship to Marley

....

....

c) Scrooge's reaction to Marley's death

....

....

....

Revise 2

How does Scrooge act towards the following characters in Stave 1?

a) Bob Cratchit

....

....

b) Fred

....

....

c) The portly gentlemen

....

....

d) The carol singer

....

....

....

Read the following paragraph (from Stave 1).

Once upon a time – of all the good days in the year, on Christmas Eve – old Scrooge sat busy in his counting-house. It was cold, bleak, biting weather: foggy withal; and he could hear the people in the court outside go wheezing up and down, beating their hands upon their breasts, and stamping their feet upon the pavement stones to warm them. The City clocks had only just gone three, but it was quite dark already – it had not been light all day – and candles were flaring in the windows of the neighbouring offices, like ruddy smears upon the palpable brown air. The fog came pouring in at every chink and keyhole, and was so dense without, that, although the court was of the narrowest, the houses opposite were mere phantoms. To see the dingy cloud come drooping down, obscuring everything, one might have thought that nature lived hard by, and was brewing on a large scale.

Write a paragraph analysing how Dickens uses language to set the scene and create atmosphere.

....

....

....

....

....

....

....

Look at this scene and fill in the missing key quotation.

HUNDREDS OF THOUSANDS ARE IN WANT OF COMMON COMFORTS, SIR.

Extend

Look at Stave 1, where Dickens describes Scrooge going to bed before the appearance of Marley's Ghost (from 'Up Scrooge went' to '"I know him! Marley's Ghost!" and fell again.'). How does Dickens create tension in the build-up to the appearance of Marley's Ghost? Write two or three paragraphs.

Think about:

- what Scrooge hears and sees before the Ghost appears
- how Dickens uses language to present the supernatural
- the reader's reaction.

Active Learning

Make a storyboard for Stave 1. Use eight frames. In each frame, put a simple sketch of an important event from the stave and label it.

Revise 1

Below is a summary of Stave 2 with the characters' names omitted. Fill in the correct names.

The **(a)** _____ takes **(b)** _____ to revisit the past. He sees himself as a lonely boy in his old school room and is shown a visit from his sister **(c)** _____, who has come to take him home. She was the mother of his nephew **(d)** _____ . They then witness a Christmas party given by Scrooge's old boss Mr **(e)** _____ when Scrooge was an apprentice. Later, he relives the scene where he parted from his fiancée **(f)** _____. Unlike him, she has had a happy and fulfilled life.

Revise 2

Briefly explain the importance of the following incidents in the reader's understanding of Scrooge's character.

a) The appearance of the characters from fiction such as Ali Baba and Robinson Crusoe

....

....

b) His being left at the school over Christmas

....

....

c) The Fezziwigs' Christmas party

....

....

d) The breaking off of his engagement

....

....

Revise 3

Read the following descriptions of places in Stave 2. Explain how Dickens uses language to convey the atmosphere and significance of the places to Scrooge and how each setting reflects the characters associated with it.

a) Scrooge's old school

It was a large house, but one of broken fortunes: for the spacious offices were little used, their walls were damp and mossy, their windows broken, and their gates decayed … entering the dreary hall, and glancing through the open doors of many rooms, they found them poorly furnished, cold and vast.

....

b) <u>Fezziwig's office</u>

Every movable was packed off, as if it were dismissed from public life for evermore; the floor was swept and watered, the lamps were trimmed, fuel was heaped upon the fire; and the warehouse was as snug, and warm, and dry, and bright a ball-room as you would desire to see upon a winter's night.

....

....

c) <u>Belle's house</u>

They were in another scene and place; a room, not very large or handsome, but full of comfort.

....

....

Look at this scene and fill in the missing key quotation.

Stave (Chapter) 2

Extend

Look at the end of Stave 2 (from 'And now Scrooge looked on more attentively than ever' to 'he sank into a heavy sleep.'). Write two or three paragraphs about how Dickens conveys the impact on Scrooge of revisiting his past. Refer to the novel's context in your answer.

Think about:

- the contrast between Scrooge's life and that of Belle's family
- Scrooge's reaction to seeing the adult Belle
- the significance of Scrooge's failed attempt to extinguish the Ghost's flame
- Dickens' use of language.

Active Learning

Make a storyboard for Stave 2. Use eight frames. In each frame, do a simple sketch of an important event in the stave and label it.

Revise 1

Number the following key incidents from Stave 3 to show the correct order:

☐ Scrooge watches the Cratchits at Christmas dinner.

☐ Scrooge enjoys watching Fred and his family celebrating Christmas.

☐ The Ghost of Christmas Present takes Scrooge through the streets of London.

☐ The Ghost shows Ignorance and Want to Scrooge.

☐ The Ghost takes Scrooge around the country, where he sees different people celebrating Christmas.

Revise 2

Explain what Scrooge learns about how these characters see him, supporting your statement with a quotation from the text:

a) The Cratchits

_____

_____

b) Fred and his family

_____

_____

Revise 3

Read Dickens' description of Scrooge's journey through Britain in Stave 3 (from 'By this time it was getting dark' to 'had known that they delighted to remember him.').

Write a paragraph exploring how Dickens uses language to present the contrast between the world outside and the Christmas celebrations that he describes.

_____

_____

_____

_____

_____

_____

_____

_____

_____

Look at this scene and fill in the missing key quotation.

THE FOUNDER OF THE FEAST INDEED!

I WISH I HAD HIM HERE. I'D GIVE HIM A PIECE OF MY MIND ...

> **Extend**

Consider the whole of Stave 3. Write two or three paragraphs explaining how Dickens builds up a picture of life in Victorian Britain. Refer to the novel's context in your answer.

Think about:

- the events that the Ghost of Christmas Present shows to Scrooge

- the reasons for choosing to present each event

- the order in which these events are organised.

> **Active Learning**

Make a storyboard for Stave 3. Draw eight frames. In each frame, do a simple sketch of an important event in the stave and label it.

Revise 1

In Stave 4, the Ghost of Christmas Yet to Come takes Scrooge to several different places to show him the possible future. Match the settings below to the people or things that they see.

Setting

a) The Exchange

b) A shop in a poor part of London

c) Scrooge's house

d) A house in Camden Town

e) A graveyard

What Scrooge Sees

1) The Cratchit family in mourning for Tiny Tim

2) A body lying on a bed

3) Scrooge's grave

4) Businessmen discussing someone's death

5) An undertaker, a charwoman and a laundress

Revise 2

Identify the character who speaks each of the following pieces of dialogue and explain what it tells us about his or her attitude to Scrooge.

Quotation	Character	Attitude
a) 'It's a judgement on him.'		
b) 'We may sleep tonight with light hearts, Caroline!'		
c) 'Old Scratch has got his own at last, hey?'		

Revise 3

Look at the descriptions in Stave 4 of Scrooge's deathbed (from 'He recoiled in terror' to 'why they were so restless and disturbed, Scrooge did not dare think.') and Tiny Tim's deathbed (from 'He broke down all at once' to 'and went down again quite happy.').

Write a paragraph exploring how Dickens uses language to show the contrast between the two scenes. Use at least one short quotation from each extract.

Extend

Consider the whole of Stave 4. Write two or three paragraphs explaining how Dickens uses language and structure to convey Scrooge's gradual realisation that he is being shown the aftermath of his own death.

Think about:

- the events that the Ghost of Christmas Yet to Come shows to Scrooge
- the importance of these events and Scrooge's reaction to them
- the order in which the events are organised.

Active Learning

Make a storyboard for Stave 4. Draw eight frames. In each frame, do a simple sketch of an important event in the stave and label it.

Look at this scene and fill in the missing key quotation.

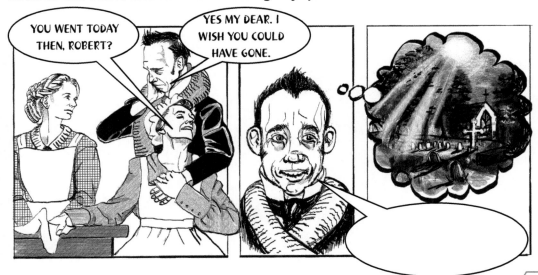

Revise 1

Read the following extract from Stave 5.

> 'I will live in the Past, the Present and the Future!' Scrooge repeated as he scrambled out of bed. 'The Spirits of all three shall strive within me. Oh, Jacob Marley! Heaven and the Christmas Time be praised for this! I say it on my knees, old Jacob; on my knees!'

Explain what Scrooge means by living in:

a) The Past

_____

_____

b) The Present

_____

_____

c) The Future

_____

_____

Revise 2

Briefly describe how Scrooge behaved towards the following at the beginning of the novel and how he makes up for his behaviour in Stave 5.

a) Bob Cratchit

_____

_____

_____

b) Fred

_____

_____

_____

c) The charity collectors

_____

_____

_____

Re-read Stave 5 (from 'He was so fluttered and so glowing' to 'Oh, glorious, glorious!').

Write a paragraph analysing how Dickens uses language and literary techniques to convey Scrooge's mood in this passage. Try to use appropriate subject terminology in your answer.

....

....

....

....

....

....

....

....

Look at this scene and fill in the missing key quotation.

IT WAS ALWAYS SAID OF HIM ...

MAY THAT BE TRULY SAID OF US, AND ALL OF US!

Extend

Consider the whole of Stave 5. Write two or three paragraphs exploring how Dickens uses language and structure to show that Scrooge has learnt from his experiences and to show his readers how they too might embrace the spirit of Christmas.

Think about:

- the changes in Scrooge's feelings and behaviour
- the lessons that Dickens might want the reader to learn from his story
- the novel's context.

Active Learning

Make a storyboard for Stave 5. Draw eight frames. In each frame, do a simple sketch of an important event in the stave and label it.

Revise 1

Dickens uses all of the following narrative techniques in *A Christmas Carol*. Briefly explain the meaning of each term.

a) Exposition (in Stave 1)

....

....

b) Cliffhanger (Stave 3)

....

....

c) Flashback (Stave 2)

....

....

d) Circular structure

....

....

Revise 2

Dickens is an 'intrusive narrator'. Look at the following quotations, where he speaks directly to the reader, and explain what effect they have on the reader.

a)

> There is no doubt that Marley was dead. This must be distinctly understood, or nothing wonderful can come of the story I am going to relate. (Stave 1)

....

....

b)

> What would I not have given to be one of them! (Stave 2)

....

....

c)

> May that be truly said of us, and all of us! (Stave 5)

....

....

Write a paragraph exploring why Dickens called his novel *A Christmas Carol* and chose to call his chapters 'staves'.

....

....

....

....

....

....

....

Look at this scene and fill in the missing key quotation.

AND SO, AS TINY TIM OBSERVED ...

Extend

Considering the novel as a whole, write two or three paragraphs about how Dickens structures the novel to involve the reader in Scrooge's story.

Think about:

- the stages in Scrooge's development
- how these stages are reflected in the novel's organisation
- how Dickens uses structural features to tell the story.

Active Learning

Create a storyboard summarising the main events of the novel with appropriate illustrations. Try to limit yourself to ten frames.

Revise 1

Indicate whether the following statements are true or false.

a) Dickens experienced poverty when his father was sent to debtors' prison.

....

b) *A Christmas Carol* was Dickens' first novel.

....

c) Dickens had a large family.

....

d) Dickens campaigned on social issues.

....

Revise 2

a) What was Dickens' motivation for writing *A Christmas Carol*?

....

....

....

....

b) Why did he decide to write a story rather than a pamphlet?

....

....

....

....

....

Choose one section of *A Christmas Carol* which you think might have been influenced by events in Dickens' own life and write a paragraph explaining how.

_____

_____

_____

_____

_____

_____

_____

_____

_____

_____

Extend

Considering the novel as a whole, write two or three paragraphs exploring how Dickens uses the genre of the ghost story to put across his message.

Think about:

- the messages he is trying to convey
- how each Ghost presents his ideas
- how using the Ghosts helps in the presentation of these ideas.

Active Learning

Use the internet to research a little bit more about Dickens' life and ideas.

Revise 1

Which TWO of the following events in the novel do NOT take place in London?

a) Scrooge's 'death' ☐

b) Scrooge's lonely Christmas at school ☐

c) Scrooge sending the turkey to the Cratchits ☐

d) The lighthouse keepers' Christmas ☐

Revise 2

Read the following description of London at Christmas (from Stave 3).

> The sky was gloomy, and the shortest streets were choked up with a dingy mist, half thawed, half frozen, whose heavier particles descended in a shower of sooty atoms, as if all the chimneys in Great Britain had, by one consent, caught fire, and were blazing away to their dear hearts' content.

Highlight the following features of the description in different colours:

a) three adjectives that convey the darkness and filth of the city

b) an example of personification, suggesting the energy of industrial Britain.

Read Dickens' description of London at Christmas in Stave 3 (from 'For the people who were shovelling away on the housetops' to 'And so it was! God love it, so it was!').

Write a paragraph exploring how Dickens uses language to present a positive picture of life in London.

_____

_____

_____

_____

_____

_____

_____

_____

_____

_____

_____

_____

_____

Extend

Think about the whole novel and choose two sections from it that you think show contrasting aspects of Victorian London.

Write two or three paragraphs explaining how Dickens presents the differences between them and what they tell us about his feelings about the city. Write about:

- the two sections you have chosen
- the differences between them
- how Dickens presents those differences.

Active Learning

Use the internet to research Victorian London. Collect some pictures of scenes from Victorian London and use them as the basis of a learning poster featuring quotations about the city taken from the novel.

Revise 1

Think about the following characters: Mrs Dilber, Mrs Fezziwig, the portly gentlemen, Peter Cratchit and the sailors. Which of them would you describe as:

a) Male and middle class ....

b) Female and middle class ....

c) Lower middle class or respectable working class ....

d) Male and working class ....

e) Female and working class ....

Revise 2

What do the following quotations suggest about the role of women in Victorian society?

a)
> Mrs Cratchit entered – flushed but smiling proudly – with the pudding … (Stave 3)

....

....

....

b)
> In came the three Miss Fezziwigs, beaming and lovable. In came the six young followers whose hearts they broke. (Stave 2)

....

....

....

c)
> '… can even I believe that you would choose a dowerless girl?' (Stave 2)

....

....

....

....

Read the following description of the Cratchits (from Stave 3).

> Then up rose Mrs Cratchit, Cratchit's wife, dressed out but poorly in a twice-turned gown, but brave in ribbons, which are cheap, and make a goodly show for sixpence; and she laid the cloth, assisted by Belinda Cratchit, second of her daughters, also brave in ribbons; while Master Peter Cratchit plunged a fork into the saucepan of potatoes, and, getting the corners of his monstrous shirt collar (Bob's private property, conferred upon his son and heir in honour of the day) into his mouth, rejoiced to find himself so gallantly attired, and yearned to show his linen in the fashionable Parks.

Write a paragraph exploring what the passage tells the reader about the Cratchits' social status.

_____

_____

_____

_____

_____

_____

_____

_____

_____

_____

Extend

Focusing on two characters from the novel, write two or three paragraphs about how the role and status of women in 19th-century Britain are reflected in *A Christmas Carol*. Think about:

- what your two characters do and say
- how they are described
- differences and similarities between them.

Active Learning

Create a learning poster featuring all the female characters in *A Christmas Carol*. You could do a sketch of each, with a quotation and a brief explanation of her role in the novel.

Revise 1

Who are the poor? For each of the following, write a sentence explaining why some people might consider them poor and a sentence explaining why others might not.

a) The Cratchits

....

....

b) Belle (when she breaks off her engagement)

....

....

c) The laundress and the charwoman

....

....

Revise 2

Find and copy a brief quotation which expresses the plight of poor people from the following parts of the novel:

a) The portly gentlemen's conversation with Scrooge in Stave 1

....

....

b) The description of Ignorance and Want at the end of Stave 3

....

....

c) The description of the people who live near the pawnshop in Stave 4.

....

....

In Stave 2, Belle says to Scrooge, 'You fear the world too much.' Even for quite wealthy people, poverty was a constant threat in the 19th century and, as in Dickens' own family, comfortable lives could be suddenly turned upside-down. Write a paragraph exploring how the threat of poverty might have influenced Scrooge's behaviour.

Extend

Read the discussion between Scrooge and the portly gentlemen in Stave 1 (from '"Scrooge and Marley's, I believe"' to 'Scrooge resumed his labours with an improved opinion of himself, and in a more facetious temper than was usual with him.').

Write two or three paragraphs about the attitudes to poverty presented in this section. Think about:

- the portly gentlemen's attitude to poverty
- Scrooge's attitude to poverty
- how Dickens presents these attitudes.

Active Learning

Create a learning poster headed 'Who Are the Poor?'. List the main (human) characters in *A Christmas Carol*, from richest to poorest (with illustrations if you wish). Find a quotation that suggests something about each character's wealth or poverty.

Revise 1

Match the following definitions to the words or phrases below:

a) Understanding of right and wrong ....

b) The day on which Christ's birth is celebrated ....

c) The part of the Bible that gives accounts of Christ's life ....

d) An immoral act ....

e) Sympathetic concern for others ....

f) The rules given to Moses by God in the Old Testament ....

Sin	Compassion	The New Testament	The Ten Commandments	Morality	Christmas Day

Revise 2

Briefly explain how the following acts could be described as 'Christian'.

a) The portly gentlemen collecting for the poor (Stave 1)

....

....

....

b) Fred welcoming Scrooge to his house for Christmas (Stave 5)

....

....

....

c) Bob Cratchit and Tiny Tim going to church (Stave 4)

....

....

....

Read the following passage, taken from Stave 4, where Bob Cratchit reflects on the death of Tiny Tim.

'And I know,' said Bob, 'I know, my dears, that when we recollect how patient and how mild he was, although he was a little, little child, we shall not quarrel easily among ourselves, and forget poor Tiny Tim in doing it.'

Write a paragraph exploring how Dickens uses language to link Tiny Tim to Christ and his teachings in this passage.

....

....

....

....

....

....

....

....

....

....

Extend

Write two or three paragraphs exploring how Scrooge's changed behaviour in Stave 5 could be described as 'moral' and 'Christian'. Think about:

- what he does and says
- how Dickens describes his behaviour.

Active Learning

Draw two columns, one headed 'Moral' and the other 'Immoral'. Under each heading, list actions taken by characters in the novel, explaining why you think they are either moral or immoral. Aim for ten actions in each column.

Revise 1

Read the following description of Scrooge (from Stave 1).

> Oh! But he was a tight-fisted hand at the grindstone, Scrooge! a squeezing, wrenching, grasping, scraping, clutching, covetous old sinner! Hard and sharp as flint, from which no steel had ever struck out generous fire: secret, and self-contained, and solitary as an oyster. The cold within him froze his old features, nipped his pointed nose, shrivelled his cheek, stiffened his gait; made his eyes red, his thin lips blue; and spoke out shrewdly in his grating voice.

Highlight the following features of the description in different colours:

a) seven adjectives that convey Scrooge's meanness

b) a simile that shows his closed and lonely personality

c) a metaphor used to express his unfriendliness

d) six physical features affected by his nature.

Revise 2

What do the following quotations from Stave 1 suggest about Scrooge?

a)
> 'Bah!' said Scrooge. 'Humbug!'

b)
> 'Are there no prisons?' asked Scrooge.
>
> 'Plenty of prisons,' said the gentleman, laying down the pen again.
>
> 'And the Union workhouses?' demanded Scrooge. 'Are they still in operation?'

c)
> Scrooge took his melancholy dinner in his usual melancholy tavern; and having read all the newspapers, and beguiled the rest of the evening with his banker's book, went home to bed.

Re-read Stave 1 (from 'External heat and cold had little influence on Scrooge' to 'in which effort, not being a man of strong imagination, he failed.').

Write a paragraph analysing how Dickens uses language to establish Scrooge's character in this section.

....

....

....

....

....

....

....

....

Extend

Look at Stave 1, where Dickens describes Scrooge's return home after work (from 'Scrooge took his melancholy dinner' to 'trimming his candle as he went.'). Write two or three paragraphs exploring how Dickens presents Scrooge in this section.

Think about:

- the way Dickens describes Scrooge's home
- Scrooge's reaction to what he sees
- what his reactions tell the reader about his character.

Active Learning

Make a poster showing the reactions to Scrooge described in Stave 1. Look through the stave and collect five or six quotations. On one side of your page, copy out the quotations. In the middle, draw a sketch of the person (or animal) whose reaction it refers to and on the other side, state briefly what the quotation tells us.

Look at this scene and fill in the missing key quotation.

A FROSTY RIME WAS ON HIS HEAD

AND ON HIS EYEBROWS, AND HIS WIRY CHIN.

Revise 1

Read the following passage in which the Ghost of Christmas Past takes Scrooge to his old school room (from Stave 2).

> They went, the Ghost and Scrooge, across the hall, to a door at the back of the house. It opened before them and disclosed a long, bare, melancholy room, made barer still by lines of plain deal forms and desks. At one of these a lonely boy was reading near a feeble fire; and Scrooge sat down upon a form, and wept to see his poor forgotten self as he had used to be.

Highlight four words or phrases in this passage that convey Scrooge's character and situation as a boy.

Revise 2

Focusing on Stave 2, select and explain a quotation that shows Scrooge's feelings about the following characters:

a) Fan

_____

_____

b) Mr Fezziwig

_____

_____

c) Belle

_____

_____

Revise 3

Read Stave 2, where the Ghost of Christmas Past shows Scrooge his younger self at school (from '"The school is not quite deserted"' to '"Let us see another Christmas!"').

Write a paragraph analysing how Dickens shows the difference between Scrooge as a child and as an adult.

_____

_____

_____

_____

_____

_____

_____

_____

_____

Look at this scene and fill in the missing key quotation.

ASSURE ME THAT I YET MAY CHANGE THESE SHADOWS YOU HAVE SHOWN ME BY AN ALTERED LIFE?

EBENEZER SCROOGE

> **Extend**

Look at the end of Stave 4, where the Ghost of Christmas Yet to Come takes Scrooge to the graveyard (from 'He joined it once again' to 'It shrunk, collapsed and dwindled down into a bedpost.').

Write two or three paragraphs explaining how Dickens shows how much Scrooge has changed.

Think about:

- the ways in which he has changed during the course of the novel
- the impact of seeing the grave
- how Dickens uses language and structure to convey how much he has changed.

> **Active Learning**

Create a learning poster showing how Scrooge changes between the beginning and the end of the novel.

On one side of the poster, headed 'Before', you could draw your impression of Scrooge at the beginning of the novel with an appropriate quotation. On the other side ('After'), you could draw Scrooge at the end of the novel, also with a quotation. Add examples of contrasting behaviour and attitudes before and after his encounters with the spirits.

Revise 1

Find quotations from Stave 1 to illustrate the following aspects of Marley's character:

a) His ghost is terrifying

b) In life, he was very like Scrooge

c) As a ghost, he shows remorse

Revise 2

What do the following quotations from Stave 2 tell us about the Ghost of Christmas Past?

a)

> … from the crown of its head there sprang a bright clear jet of light …

b)

> 'Your reclamation then. Take heed!'

c)

> But the relentless Ghost pinioned him in both his arms, and forced him observe what happened next.

d)

> … though Scrooge pressed it down with all his force, he could not hide the light, which streamed from under it in an unbroken flood upon the ground.

Re-read Stave 1 (from 'The Ghost, on hearing this, set up another cry' to '"You were always a good friend to me," said Scrooge. "Thankee!"'). Write a paragraph exploring how Dickens uses Marley's Ghost to show the immorality of his and Scrooge's way of life.

....

....

....

....

....

....

....

....

Extend

Read the description of the Ghost of Christmas Past at the beginning of Stave 2 (from 'It was a strange figure' to '"Rise! And walk with me!"').

Write two or three paragraphs exploring the function and significance of the Ghost of Christmas Past.

Think about:

- how Dickens describes the Ghost
- the way Scrooge reacts to the Ghost
- the Ghost's role in changing Scrooge.

Link your comments to the context of the novel.

Active Learning

Create two posters, one for Marley's Ghost and one for the Ghost of Christmas Past. Draw the ghosts, including as much detail as you can from Dickens' descriptions of them. Using arrows, label the details with explanations of their significance, for example, 'The cash boxes show Marley's obsession with money.'

Look at this scene and fill in the missing key quotation.

Revise 1

Read the following description of the Ghost of Christmas Yet to Come (from Stave 4).

> It was shrouded in a deep black garment, which concealed its head, its face, its form, and left nothing of it visible, save one outstretched hand. But for this, it would have been difficult to detach its figure from the night, and separate it from the darkness by which it was surrounded.

Highlight four words in the description which link the phantom to death.

Revise 2

Explain the significance of the following quotations, taken from the description of the Ghost of Christmas Present in Stave 3.

a)
> … a glowing torch, in shape not unlike Plenty's horn …

b)
> … a holly wreath, set here and there with shining icicles …

c)
> … its genial face, its sparkling eye, its open hand, its cheery voice, its unconstrained demeanour, and its joyful air …

d)
> … no sword was in it, and the ancient sheath was eaten up with rust …

Think about Stave 4. Why do you think the Ghost of Christmas Yet to Come never shows its face and never speaks?

....

....

....

....

....

....

....

....

....

Extend

Focus on Stave 3.

Write two or three paragraphs exploring the role and importance of the Ghost of Christmas Present in the novel. Refer to the novel's context within your answer.

Think about:

- how the Ghost is described
- what it does and what it shows to Scrooge
- what it represents.

Look at this scene and fill in the missing key quotation.

IN EASY STATE UPON THIS COUCH THERE SAT ...

Active Learning

Create a learning poster about the Ghost of Christmas Present. In the centre, sketch the Ghost as described by Dickens, including all the objects with which he is surrounded. Label these and give a brief explanation of the significance of each.

Revise 1

Which member of the Cratchit family is referred to in each of the following quotations?

a) '... he bore a little crutch, and had his limbs supported by an iron frame!' ....

b) '... she didn't like to see [Bob] disappointed, if it were only in joke ...' ....

c) '... might have known, and very likely did, the inside of a pawnbroker's ...' ....

d) '... dressed out but poorly in a twice-turned gown ...' ....

Revise 2

Read this description of Bob Cratchit from Stave 1.

> The office was closed in a twinkling, and the clerk, with the long ends of his white comforter dangling below his waist (for he boasted no great coat), went down a slide on Cornhill, at the end of a lane of boys, twenty times in honour of its being Christmas Eve, and then ran home to Camden Town as hard as he could pelt, to play at blindman's buff.

Write a paragraph exploring the impression of Bob Cratchit that this passage gives the reader.

....

....

....

....

....

....

....

Revise 3

Think about Staves 3 and 4. Write a paragraph summarising how Dickens presents Bob Cratchit as a father.

....

....

....

....

....

....

....

....

....

....

....

Extend

'Spirit,' said Scrooge with an interest he had never felt before, 'tell me if Tiny Tim will live.'

'I see a vacant seat,' replied the Ghost, 'in the poor chimney corner, and a crutch without an owner, carefully preserved. If these shadows remain unaltered by the Future, the child will die.' (Stave 3)

Write two or three paragraphs exploring the importance of Tiny Tim in the novel. Think about:

- what he says and does
- how Dickens presents him
- his effect on Scrooge.

Look at this scene and fill in the missing key quotation.

IT SHOULD BE CHRISTMAS DAY, I AM SURE ...

... ON WHICH ONE DRINKS THE HEALTH OF SUCH AN ODIOUS, STINGY, HARD, UNFEELING MAN AS MR SCROOGE.

Active Learning

Create a family tree for the Cratchits, clearly showing their relationships to each other. Under their names, include a brief quotation about each one.

Revise 1

a) Circle the FOUR adjectives that most accurately describe Fred.

generous   energetic   unfriendly   selfish   warm   ambitious   playful

b) Circle the FOUR adjectives that most accurately describe Fan.

delicate   cold   loving   overbearing   unforgiving   optimistic   eager

Revise 2

Read the following quotations and explain how they illustrate differences between Scrooge and either Fan or Fred.

a)

> It opened and a little girl, much younger than the boy, came darting in, and, putting her arms about his neck, and often kissing him, addressed him as her 'dear, dear brother.' (Stave 2)

b)

> His nephew left the room without an angry word, notwithstanding. He stopped at the outer door to bestow the greetings of the season on the clerk, who, cold as he was, was warmer than Scrooge; for he returned them cordially. (Stave 1)

Revise 3

Read the following extract from Stave 1, describing the arrival of Fred at Scrooge's counting house.

> 'A merry Christmas, uncle! God save you!' cried a cheerful voice. It was the voice of Scrooge's nephew, who came upon him so quickly that this was the first intimation he had of his approach.
>
> 'Bah!' said Scrooge. 'Humbug!'
>
> He had so heated himself with rapid walking in the fog and frost, this nephew of Scrooge's, that he was all in a glow; his face was ruddy and handsome; his eyes sparkled, and his breath smoked again.

Write a paragraph exploring how Dickens uses language to give a positive first impression of Fred.

....

....

....

....

....

....

....

....

Look at this scene and fill in the missing key quotation.

WHY DID YOU GET MARRIED?

Extend

'She died a woman,' said the Ghost, 'and had, as I think, children.'

'One child,' Scrooge returned.

'True,' said the Ghost. 'Your nephew!'

Scrooge seemed uneasy in his mind; and answered briefly, 'Yes.' (Stave 2)

Write two or three paragraphs exploring how Scrooge's observations of Fan and Fred are instrumental in changing him. Think about:

- what the Ghosts show him
- the impressions these visions have on Scrooge
- how Dickens presents Fan and Fred.

Active Learning

Write a diary entry for Fan describing her conversation with her father and her feelings about being sent to bring Scrooge home.

Revise 1

What do the following quotes from Stave 2 suggest about Mr Fezziwig's character?

a)

> … a comfortable, oily, rich, fat, jovial voice …

b)

> … skipping down from the high desk with wonderful agility …

c)

> Mr and Mrs Fezziwig took their stations, one on either side of the door, and, shaking hands with every person individually as he or she went out, wished him or her a Merry Christmas.

Revise 2

Read the following passage (from Stave 2).

> There was an eager, greedy, restless motion in the eye, which showed the passion that had taken root, and where the shadow of the growing tree would fall.
>
> He was not alone, but sat by the side of a fair young girl in a mourning dress: in whose eyes there were tears, which sparkled in the light that shone out of the Ghost of Christmas Past.

Highlight the following features of the description in different colours:

a) a triplet of adjectives that show how Scrooge has changed since he worked for Fezziwig

b) a phrase that tells us that Belle has recently been bereaved

c) a noun that suggests bereavement but might also indicate her feelings about Scrooge.

Read the following quote (from Stave 2).

'No,' said Scrooge, 'No. I should like to be able to say a word or two to my clerk just now! That's all.'

Write a paragraph explaining why re-living the Fezziwigs' party makes Scrooge think about Bob Cratchit.

....

....

....

....

....

....

....

Extend

Look at the end of Stave 2, where the Ghost shows Scrooge what has happened to Belle (from 'They were in another scene and place' to '"Remove me!" Scrooge exclaimed. "I cannot bear it!"'). Write two or three paragraphs explaining how Dickens presents the contrast between Belle's life and Scrooge's life. Refer to the novel's context within your answer.

Think about:

- the way Dickens describes Belle and her family

- Scrooge's reaction to what he sees

- the importance of this section in Scrooge's development.

Look at this scene and fill in the missing key quotation.

Active Learning

Divide a piece of paper into four or create a table on your computer (two columns, two rows). In the top two rows, put all the words and phrases (including quotations) you can think of to describe Scrooge and Belle as they were when they parted. In the bottom two put words and phrases that describe them when they are older (as at the end of Stave 2).

Revise 1

Indicate whether the following statements are true or false.

a) Christmas is seen as a time to think of those in need. ....

b) Dickens did not approve of having parties at Christmas. ....

c) The tradition of decorating the house with holly, ivy and mistletoe dates from pre-Christian times. ....

d) Going to church is an important part of celebrating Christmas. ....

e) Victorians fasted during Christmas. ....

f) Carols are songs on religious themes sung at Christmas. ....

Revise 2

Read the following quote from Stave 3 and then answer the questions.

> 'Is there a peculiar flavour in what you sprinkle from your torch?' asked Scrooge.

a) What makes Scrooge ask this question?

....

....

b) What is the Ghost of Christmas Past's answer?

....

....

c) What does the Ghost mean by his answer?

....

....

Revise 3

Read what Fred says about Christmas in Stave 1.

> 'But I am sure I have always thought of Christmas-time, when it has come round – apart from the veneration due to its sacred name and origin, if anything belonging to it can be apart from that – as a good time; a kind, forgiving, charitable, pleasant time; the only time I know of, in the long calendar of the year, when men and women seem by one consent to open up their shut-up hearts freely, and to think of people below them as if they really were fellow-passengers to the grave, and not another race of creatures bound on other journeys.

Write a paragraph exploring how Dickens uses language to convey Fred's (and his own) attitude to Christmas.

....

....

....

....

....

....

....

Look at this scene and fill in the missing key quotation.

ONCE OR TWICE, WHEN THERE WERE ANGRY WORDS BETWEEN SOME DINNER CARRIERS ...

Extend

Focus on Stave 3. Write two or three paragraphs exploring what Dickens means by the spirit of Christmas and how he conveys it here.

Think about:

- examples of the spirit of Christmas

- what these examples tell us about what Dickens means by the spirit of Christmas

- the context of the novel.

Active Learning

Look for images of Victorian Christmas cards. Use one as the focal point of a learning poster and, around it, place words and images which reflect the idea of 'the Spirit of Christmas', as shown in the novel.

Revise 1

Using the words below, fill in the gaps in this paragraph.

| greed | earn | consequences | marry | miser | loves | dishonestly | charity |

Money is a theme that runs through the novel. Scrooge has a lot of money but is a
(a) _____ and does not spend much. He accuses his nephew of not having enough
money to **(b)** _____. He refuses to give money to the men who are collecting for
(c) _____. Marley's Ghost warns him of the consequence of **(d)** _____.
He is rejected by Belle because he **(e)** _____ money more than he loves her.
The Cratchits make the most of the little money they **(f)** _____, while the people in
the pawnshop get money **(g)** _____. Want is a terrible warning of the
(h) _____ of having no money at all.

Revise 2

Read the following quote from Stave 1.

> He had been quite familiar with one old ghost in a white waistcoat, with a monstrous iron safe attached to its ankle, who cried piteously at being unable to assist a wretched woman with an infant, whom it saw below upon a doorstep. (Stave 1)

Highlight the following features of the description in different colours:

a) a noun phrase that symbolises the love of money

b) an emotive adverb that suggests the Ghost's suffering

c) an emotive adjective that suggests the woman's poverty.

Revise 3

Read the following paragraph from Stave 4.

> Scrooge listened to this dialogue in horror. As they sat grouped about their spoil, in the scanty light afforded by the old man's lamp, he viewed them with a detestation and disgust which could hardly have been greater, though they had been obscure demons, marketing the corpse itself.

Write a paragraph exploring how Dickens uses language to convey Scrooge's revulsion at the greed of others and the irony of his reaction to it.

_____

_____

_____

_____

....

....

....

....

Look at this scene and fill in the missing key quotation.

Extend

Focus on the part of Stave 2 where Scrooge watches his younger self with Belle (from 'This was not addressed to Scrooge' to 'Show me no more!'). Write two or three paragraphs exploring how Dickens presents the effect of avarice.

Think about:

- the effect of Scrooge's avarice on his character and his relationship with Belle
- how Dickens uses language to convey this
- the context of the novel.

Active Learning

Create a learning poster on the theme of 'greed and avarice'. Place all the characters you can think of along a line from the greediest to the least greedy and explain why you have placed them there.

Revise 1

Explain in a few words what is meant by:

a) Ignorance

....

....

b) Want

....

....

Revise 2

a) Why do you think Dickens personifies Ignorance and Want as children?

....

....

b) Why are they shown to Scrooge by the Ghost of Christmas Present (rather than one of the other spirits)?

....

....

c) What does the Ghost mean by 'They are Man's'?

....

....

d) What is the significance of the word 'Doom' on Ignorance's brow?

....

....

Read the following passage from Stave 3.

> Where graceful youth should have filled their features out, and touched them with its freshest tints, a stale and shrivelled hand, like that of age, had pinched and twisted them, and pulled them to shreds. Where angels might have sat enthroned, devils lurked, and glared out menacing.

Write a paragraph explaining how Dickens uses language in the passage above to present the contrast between the Victorian ideal of childhood and the reality.

....

....

....

....

Extend

Focus on the end of Stave 3 (from 'The chimes were ringing the three-quarters past eleven at that moment' to 'The bell struck twelve.').

Write two or three paragraphs exploring how Dickens presents Ignorance and Want and his reasons for including them in the novel.

Think about:

- the ideas that Dickens presents in this section
- how he presents these ideas
- the social and historical context of the novel.

Active Learning

Research education in Victorian times, particularly the 'ragged schools' and Dickens' involvement with them.

Look at this scene and fill in the missing key quotation.

Revise 1

Match the following families with the appropriate descriptions.

a) Scrooge's family

b) The Cratchits

c) The Fezziwigs

d) The Miner's family

e) Belle's family

f) Fred's family

1. A middle-class family including a husband, a wife and a lot of young children

2. A working-class family of four generations

3. A widower with two children

4. A poor but respectable married couple with children of various ages

5. A young married couple plus the wife's sisters

6. A well-off couple and their grown-up daughters

Revise 2

Read the following passage, from Stave 3, where Scrooge is watching Belle and her family.

> And now Scrooge looked on more attentively than ever, when the master of the house, having his daughter leaning fondly on him, sat down with her and her mother at his own fireside …

Highlight the following features of the passage in different colours:

a) a noun phrase that suggests the traditional role of the Victorian father

b) two nouns with possessive pronouns that define family relationships

c) an adverb that shows the daughter's love for her father

d) a phrase that symbolises the warmth and comfort of family life.

Revise 3

Read what Fan says to Ebenezer when she comes to take him home from school in Stave 2.

> 'Father is so much kinder than he used to be, that Home's like Heaven! He spoke so gently to me one dear night when I was going to bed, that I was not afraid to ask him once more if you might come home; and he said Yes, you should; and sent me in a coach to bring you.'

Write a paragraph exploring what we learn from this passage and its context about Scrooge's childhood.

Extend

Think about the whole novel. Focus on TWO families that Scrooge is shown by the ghosts. Write two or three paragraphs exploring how Dickens uses these families to convey ideas about family life.

Consider:

- the relationships within each family and how family members act towards each other
- how Dickens presents the families
- the social and historical context of the novel.

Active Learning

Use the internet to find out a bit more about Victorian ideas about families. Think about how these ideas are reflected in the novel and how they differ from modern ideas.

Look at this scene and fill in the missing key quotation.

AN OLD, OLD MAN AND WOMAN

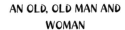

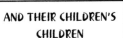

Revise 1

Match the following quotations to the appropriate comments:

a) '"I don't mind going if a lunch is provided," observed the gentleman with the excresence on his nose. "But I must be fed if I make one."'

b) '"What do you call wasting of it?" asked old Joe.

"Putting it on him to be buried in, to be sure," replied the woman with a laugh.'

c) 'She was a mild and patient creature, if her face spoke the truth; but she was thankful in her soul to hear it …'

1. Scrooge's charwoman reveals that she has stolen his shirt, showing her lack of respect for the dead and her contempt for Scrooge.

2. Caroline, who is in debt to Scrooge, reacts instinctively to news of his death.

3. Dickens uses humour to show how little Scrooge's acquaintances care about his death.

Revise 2

Read the following passage, from Stave 4, where Dickens addresses Death.

> Oh cold, cold, rigid, dreadful Death, set up thine altar here, and dress it with such terrors as thou hast at thy command: for this is thy dominion! But of the loved, revered, and honoured head thou canst not turn one hair to thy dread purposes, or make one feature odious.

Write a paragraph exploring how Dickens uses language to express ideas about death.

_____

_____

_____

_____

_____

_____

Read the following description of Tim's deathbed from Stave 4.

> He left the room, and went up-stairs into the room above, which was lighted cheerfully, and hung with Christmas. There was a chair set close beside the child, and there were signs of someone having been there lately. Poor Bob sat down in it, and, when he had thought a little and composed himself, he kissed the little face. He was reconciled to what had happened and went down again quite happy.

Write a paragraph explaining your reaction, as a reader, to this passage.

....

....

....

....

....

....

Look at this scene and fill in the missing key quotation.

MRS CRATCHIT KISSED HIM, HIS DAUGHTERS KISSED HIM ...

... THE TWO YOUNG CRATCHITS KISSED HIM, AND PETER AND HIMSELF SHOOK HANDS.

Extend

Focus on Stave 4. Write two or three paragraphs exploring the ways in which Dickens presents reactions to the death of Scrooge and to the death of Tiny Tim. Try to refer to the novel's context within your answer.

Think about:

- the differences between how people react to the two deaths
- how Dickens presents these reactions
- how he uses these differences to explore ideas about death.

Active Learning

Imagine that the reformed Scrooge has just died. Write his obituary. Include a brief summary of his life and praise for his character and achievements, including at least five quotations from the novel.

Revise 1

Look at the part of Stave 1 where the portly gentlemen visit Scrooge. Select a quotation that:

a) explains the gentlemen's motive for collecting for the poor

b) implies that Scrooge thinks he is doing enough by paying tax

c) makes it clear that Scrooge feels he has no responsibility for the poor.

Revise 2

In what sense might Scrooge be held responsible for the following?

a) His own loneliness

b) Tiny Tim's condition

c) The existence of Ignorance and Want

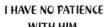

Focusing on the idea of responsibility, explain what Marley's Ghost means in Stave 1 when he says:

'Mankind was my business. The common welfare was my business; charity, mercy, forbearance, and benevolence were, all, my business.'

....

....

....

....

Look at this scene and fill in the missing key quotation.

Extend

'They are Man's,' said the Spirit. (Stave 3)

Write two or three paragraphs exploring what the Spirit means when he says that Ignorance and Want are 'Man's'. Try to include references to historical and social context in your answer.

Think about:

- the origin of poverty and ignorance and who is responsible for creating them
- the consequence of not taking responsibility for them, as expressed by the Spirit
- how Dickens presents these ideas.

Active Learning

Make a learning poster on the theme of responsibility. Place all the characters you can think of who display responsibility or lack of responsibility along a line, with the least responsible (Scrooge?) at one end and the most responsible at the other.

Revise 1

Number the three stages of Scrooge's redemption to show the correct order.

☐ Scrooge is shown what will happen if he does not reform and he decides to change.

☐ Scrooge relives his past and starts to understand what he has done wrong.

☐ Scrooge is redeemed and is a changed man.

Revise 2

Read the following quote from Marley's Ghost in Stave 1.

> 'This is no light part of my penance,' pursued the Ghost. 'I am here tonight to warn you that you have yet a chance and hope of escaping my fate. A chance and a hope of my procuring, Ebenezer.'

Highlight the following features of the quote in different colours:

a) an abstract noun that shows Marley is paying for his sins

b) repetition of two abstract nouns suggesting the possibility of Scrooge being redeemed

c) the use of litotes (understatement) to suggest that the Ghost's penance is very hard.

Revise 3

Focus on Stave 5. Write a paragraph explaining how Scrooge's behaviour in the final stave shows that he has been redeemed.

_____

_____

_____

_____

_____

_____

_____

Look at the following extract from Stave 4.

> 'Good Spirit,' he pursued, as down upon the ground he fell before it: 'your nature intercedes for me, and pities me. Assure me that I yet may change these shadows you have shown me by an altered life?'
>
> The kind hand trembled.

Write two or three paragraphs exploring how Dickens uses Scrooge's experiences to convey ideas about redemption.

Think about:

- what is meant by redemption
- how Scrooge is redeemed
- how Dickens presents ideas about redemption.

Active Learning

Make a learning poster showing the stages of Scrooge's redemption in pictures with appropriate brief quotations.

Look at this scene and fill in the missing key quotation.

Read the following extract from Stave 3 and then answer the question that follows.

At this point in the book, Scrooge and the Ghost of Christmas Present are watching Fred's Christmas party.

'Ha, ha!' laughed Scrooge's nephew. 'Ha, ha, ha!'

If you should happen, by any unlikely chance, to know a man more blest in a laugh than Scrooge's nephew, all I can say is, I should like to know him too. Introduce him to me, and I'll cultivate his acquaintance.

It is a fair, even-handed, noble adjustment of things, that while there is infection in disease and sorrow, there is nothing in the world so irresistibly contagious as laughter and good-humour. When Scrooge's nephew laughed in this way – holding his sides, rolling his head, and twisting his face into the most extravagant contortions – Scrooge's niece, by marriage, laughed as heartily as he. And their assembled friends, being not a bit behindhand, roared out lustily.

'Ha, ha! Ha, ha, ha, ha!'

'He said that Christmas was a humbug, as I live!' cried Scrooge's nephew. 'He believed it too!'

'More shame for him, Fred!' said Scrooge's niece, indignantly. Bless those women; they never do anything by halves. They are always in earnest.

…

'He's a comical old fellow,' said Scrooge's nephew, 'that's the truth: and not so pleasant as he might be. However, his offences carry their own punishment, and I have nothing to say against him.'

'I'm sure he is very rich, Fred,' hinted Scrooge's niece. 'At least you always tell *me* so.'

'What of that, my dear?' said Scrooge's nephew. 'His wealth is of no use to him. He don't do any good with it. He don't make himself comfortable with it. He hasn't the satisfaction of thinking – ha, ha, ha! – that he is ever going to benefit US with it.'

'I have no patience with him,' observed Scrooge's niece. Scrooge's niece's sisters, and all the other ladies, expressed the same opinion.

'Oh, I have!' said Scrooge's nephew. 'I am sorry for him; I couldn't be angry with him if I tried. Who suffers by his ill whims? Himself, always. Here, he takes it into his head to dislike us, and he won't come and dine with us. What's the consequence? He don't lose much of a dinner.'

Starting with this extract, explore how Dickens presents Fred as a contrast to Scrooge.

Write about:

- how he presents Fred in this extract
- how he presents Fred in the novel as a whole.

Underline the words and phrases that show what you need to focus on to answer the first bullet point. Then annotate the extract.

Pick three or four other parts of the novel that you can refer to in answering the second bullet point.

Plan your response to the question. Try to come up with four or five ideas, linked to quotations and context (where appropriate).

Spend about five minutes on this.

> **Extend**

Write your response to the question. Spend 40–45 minutes on this.

Read the following extract from Stave 2 and then answer the question that follows.

At this point in the book, Scrooge and the Ghost of Christmas Past are watching as Belle releases Scrooge from their engagement.

> This was not addressed to Scrooge, or to any one whom he could see, but it produced an immediate effect. For again Scrooge saw himself. He was older now; a man in the prime of life. His face had not the harsh and rigid lines of later years; but it had begun to wear the signs of care and avarice. There was an eager, greedy, restless motion in the eye, which showed the passion that had taken root, and where the shadow of the growing tree would fall.
>
> He was not alone, but sat by the side of a fair young girl in a mourning-dress: in whose eyes there were tears, which sparkled in the light that shone out of the Ghost of Christmas Past.
>
> 'It matters little,' she said, softly. 'To you, very little. Another idol has displaced me; and if it can cheer and comfort you in time to come, as I would have tried to do, I have no just cause to grieve.'
>
> 'What Idol has displaced you?' he re-joined.
>
> 'A golden one.'
>
> 'This is the even-handed dealing of the world!' he said. 'There is nothing on which it is so hard as poverty; and there is nothing it professes to condemn with such severity as the pursuit of wealth!'
>
> 'You fear the world too much,' she answered, gently. 'All your other hopes have merged into the hope of being beyond the chance of its sordid reproach. I have seen your nobler aspirations fall off one by one, until the master-passion, Gain, engrosses you. Have I not?'
>
> 'What then?' he retorted. 'Even if I have grown so much wiser, what then? I am not changed towards you.'
>
> She shook her head.
>
> 'Am I?'
>
> 'Our contract is an old one. It was made when we were both poor and content to be so, until, in good season, we could improve our worldly fortune by our patient industry. You *are* changed. When it was made, you were another man.'
>
> 'I was a boy,' he said impatiently.

Starting with this extract, explain how Dickens writes about how Scrooge changes from boyhood up to the death of Marley.

Write about:

- how he presents Scrooge in this extract
- how he presents Scrooge in the novel as a whole.

Underline the words and phrases that show what you need to focus on to answer the first bullet point. Then annotate the extract.

Revise 2

Pick three or four other parts of the novel that you can refer to in answering the second bullet point.

Plan your response to the question. Try to come up with four or five ideas, linked to quotations and context (where appropriate).

Spend about five minutes on this.

Extend

Write your response to the question. Spend 40–45 minutes on this.

Read the following extract from Stave 3 and then answer the question that follows.

At this point in the book, the Ghost of Christmas Present is showing Scrooge how different groups of people celebrate Christmas.

> 'What place is this?' asked Scrooge.
>
> 'A place where miners live, who labour in the bowels of the earth,' returned the Spirit. 'But they know me. See!'
>
> A light shone from the window of a hut, and swiftly they advanced towards it. Passing through the wall of mud and stone, they found a cheerful company assembled round a glowing fire. An old, old man and woman, with their children and their children's children, and another generation beyond that, all decked out gaily in their holiday attire. The old man, in a voice that seldom rose above the howling of the wind upon the barren waste, was singing them a Christmas song: it had been a very old song when he was a boy; and from time to time they all joined in the chorus. So surely as they raised their voices, the old man got quite blithe and loud; and so surely as they stopped, his vigour sank again.
>
> The Spirit did not tarry here, but bade Scrooge hold his robe, and, passing on above the moor, sped whither? Not to sea? To sea. To Scrooge's horror, looking back, he saw the last of the land, a frightful range of rocks, behind them; and his ears were deafened by the thundering of water, as it rolled and roared, and raged among the dreadful caverns it had worn, and fiercely tried to undermine the earth.
>
> Built upon a dismal reef of sunken rocks, some league or so from shore, on which the waters chafed and dashed, the wild year through, there stood a solitary lighthouse. Great heaps of sea-weed clung to its base, and storm-birds – born of the wind, one might suppose, as sea-weed of the water – rose and fell about it, like the waves they skimmed.
>
> But even here, two men who watched the light had made a fire, that through the loophole in the thick stone wall shed out a ray of brightness on the awful sea. Joining their horny hands over the rough table at which they sat, they wished each other Merry Christmas in their can of grog; and one of them – the elder, too, with his face all damaged and scarred with hard weather, as the figure-head of an old ship might be – struck up a sturdy song that was like a gale in itself.

Starting with this extract, explain what is meant by the spirit of Christmas and how Dickens writes about it. Write about:

- how he writes about the spirit of Christmas in the extract
- how he writes about the spirit of Christmas in the novel as a whole.

Underline the words and phrases that show what you need to focus on to answer the first bullet point. Then annotate the extract.

Pick three or four other parts of the novel that you can refer to in answering the second bullet point.

Plan your response to the question. Try to come up with four or five ideas, linked to quotations and context (where appropriate).

Spend about five minutes on this.

Extend

Write your response to the question.

Spend 40–45 minutes on this.

Read the following extract from Stave 4 and then answer the question that follows.

At this point in the book, the Cratchits are mourning the death of Tiny Tim.

They drew about the fire, and talked; the girls and mother working still. Bob told them of the extraordinary kindness of Mr Scrooge's nephew, whom he had scarcely seen but once, and who, meeting him in the street that day, and seeing that he looked a little – 'just a little down you know,' said Bob, inquired what had happened to distress him. 'On which,' said Bob, 'for he is the pleasantest-spoken gentleman you ever heard, I told him. "I am heartily sorry for it, Mr Cratchit," he said, "and heartily sorry for your good wife." By-the-bye, how he ever knew *that*, I don't know.'

'Knew what, my dear?'

'Why, that you were a good wife,' replied Bob.

'Everybody knows that,' said Peter.

'Very well observed, my boy!' cried Bob. 'I hope they do. "Heartily sorry," he said, "for your good wife. If I can be of service to you in any way," he said, giving me his card, "that's where I live. Pray come to me." Now, it wasn't,' cried Bob, 'for the sake of anything he might be able to do for us, so much as for his kind way, that this was quite delightful. It really seemed as if he had known our Tiny Tim, and felt with us.'

'I'm sure he's a good soul!' said Mrs Cratchit.

'You would be surer of it, my dear,' returned Bob, 'if you saw and spoke to him. I shouldn't be at all surprised, mark what I say, if he got Peter a better situation.'

'Only hear that, Peter,' said Mrs Cratchit.

'And then,' cried one of the girls, 'Peter will be keeping company with someone, and setting up for himself.'

'Get along with you!' retorted Peter, grinning.

'It's just as likely as not,' said Bob, 'one of these days; though there's plenty of time for that, my dear. But however and whenever we part from one another, I am sure we shall none of us forget poor Tiny Tim – shall we – or this first parting that there was among us?'

'Never, father!' cried they all.

'And I know,' said Bob, 'I know, my dears, that when we recollect how patient and how mild he was; although he was a little, little child; we shall not quarrel easily among ourselves, and forget poor Tiny Tim in doing it.'

'No, never, father!' they all cried again.

'I am very happy' said little Bob, 'I am very happy!'

Mrs Cratchit kissed him, his daughters kissed him, the two young Cratchits kissed him, and Peter and himself shook hands. Spirit of Tiny Tim, thy childish essence was from God!

Starting with this extract, how far do you think that Dickens presents the Cratchits as the ideal family? Write about:

- how he presents the Cratchit family in this extract
- how he presents the Cratchit family in the novel as a whole.

Underline the words and phrases that show what you need to focus on to answer the first bullet point. Then annotate the extract.

Pick three or four other parts of the novel that you can refer to in answering the second bullet point.

Plan your response to the question. Try to come up with four or five ideas, linked to quotations and context (where appropriate).

Spend about five minutes on this.

Extend

Write your response to the question.

Spend 40–45 minutes on this.

Read the following extract from Stave 5 and then answer the question that follows.

At this point in the book, Scrooge is waking up a changed man on Christmas morning.

Yes! And the bedpost was his own. The bed was his own, the room was his own. Best and happiest of all, the Time before him was his own, to make amends in!

'I will live in the Past, the Present and the Future!' Scrooge repeated as he scrambled out of bed. 'The Spirits of all Three shall strive within me. Oh, Jacob Marley! Heaven and the Christmas Time be praised for this! I say it on my knees, old Jacob, on my knees!'

He was so fluttered and so glowing with his good intentions that his broken voice would scarcely answer to his call. He had been sobbing violently in his conflict with the Spirit, and his face was wet with tears.

'They are not torn down,' cried Scrooge, folding one of his bed-curtains in his arms, 'they are not torn down, rings and all. They are here – I am here – the shadows of the things that would have been may be dispelled. They will be. I know they will!'

His hands were busy with his garments all this time; turning them inside out, putting them on upside down, tearing them, mislaying them, making them parties to every kind of extravagance.

'I don't know what to do!' cried Scrooge, laughing and crying in the same breath; and making a perfect Laocoon of himself with his stockings. 'I am as light as a feather. I am as happy as an angel. I am as merry as a school-boy. I am as giddy as a drunken man. A merry Christmas to everybody! A happy New Year to all the world! Hallo here! Whoop! Hallo!'

He had frisked into the sitting room, and was now standing there: perfectly winded.

'There's the saucepan that the gruel was in!' cried Scrooge, starting off again, and going round the fireplace. 'There's the door by which the Ghost of Jacob Marley entered! There's the corner where the Ghost of Christmas Present sat. There's the window where I saw the wandering Spirits! It's all right, it's all true, it all happened. Ha, ha, ha!'

Really, for a man who had been out of practice for so many years, it was a splendid laugh, a most illustrious laugh. The father of a long, long line of brilliant laughs!

Starting with this extract, explore how Dickens presents the way in which Scrooge's experiences with the Spirits change him. Write about:

- how he presents Scrooge in this extract
- how he presents Scrooge in the novel as a whole.

Underline the words and phrases that show what you need to focus on to answer the first bullet point. Then annotate the extract.

Pick three or four other parts of the novel that you can refer to in answering the second bullet point.

Plan your response to the question. Try to come up with four or five ideas, linked to quotations and context (where appropriate).

Spend about five minutes on this.

Write your response to the question.

Spend 40–45 minutes on this.

Read the following extract from Stave 1 and then answer the question that follows.

At this point in the book, Marley's Ghost is warning Scrooge of the consequences of his behaviour and telling him about the spirits that will visit him.

'Business!' cried the Ghost, wringing its hands again. 'Mankind was my business. The common welfare was my business: charity, mercy, forbearance, and benevolence were, all, my business. The dealings of my trade were but a drop of water in the comprehensive ocean of my business!'

It held up its chain at arm's length, as if that were the cause of all its unavailing grief, and flung it heavily upon the ground again.

'At this time of the rolling year,' the spectre said, 'I suffer most. Why did I walk through crowds of fellow-beings with my eyes turned down and never raise them to that blessed Star which led the Wise Men to a poor abode? Were there no poor homes to which its light would have conducted *me*?'

Scrooge was very much dismayed to hear the spectre going on at this rate, and began to quake exceedingly.

'Hear me!' cried the Ghost. 'My time is nearly gone.'

'I will,' said Scrooge. 'But don't be hard upon me! Don't be flowery, Jacob! Pray!'

'How it is that I appear before you in a shape that you can see, I may not tell. I have sat invisible beside you on many and many a day.'

It was not an agreeable idea. Scrooge shivered, and wiped the perspiration from his brow.

'That is no light part of my penance,' pursued the Ghost. 'I am here tonight to warn you that you have a chance yet and hope of escaping my fate. A chance and hope of my procuring, Ebenezer.'

'You were always a good friend to me,' said Scrooge. 'Thankee!'

'You will be haunted,' resumed the Ghost, 'by Three Spirits.'

Scrooge's countenance fell almost as low as the Ghost's had done.

'Is that the chance and hope you mentioned, Jacob?' he demanded in a faltering voice.

'It is.'

'I – I think I'd rather not,' said Scrooge.

'Without their visits,' said the Ghost, 'you cannot hope to shun the path I tread. Expect the first to-morrow when the bell tolls One.'

Starting with this extract, explore how Dickens presents ideas about sin and redemption. Write about:

- how he presents ideas about sin and redemption in this extract
- how he presents ideas about sin and redemption in the novel as a whole.

Underline the words and phrases that show what you need to focus on to answer the first bullet point. Then annotate the extract.

Pick three or four other parts of the novel that you can refer to in answering the second bullet point.

Revise 1

Plan your response to the question. Try to come up with four or five ideas, linked to quotations and context (where appropriate).

Spend about five minutes on this.

Extend

Write your response to the question.

Spend 40–45 minutes on this.

Revise 1

Match the following terms to the correct definitions.

a) adverb

b) adjective

c) verb

d) pronoun

e) abstract noun

1. a short word that replaces a noun

2. a word that modifies a noun

3. a noun that names an idea or quality

4. a word that describes a verb

5. a doing, feeling, thinking or being word

Revise 2

What kind of imagery are the following examples of?

a) 'I am as light as a feather!' _____

b) 'A frosty rime was on his head.' _____

c) Ignorance and Want _____

d) 'to see the dingy cloud come drooping down' _____

Revise 3

Answer these questions and explain the reason for each answer.

a) Who is the protagonist of *A Christmas Carol*?

_____

_____

b) What sort of narrator is Dickens?

_____

_____

c) Which stave includes exposition?

_____

_____

Revise 4

Look at the first three paragraphs of Stave 1. Give examples from these paragraphs of:

a) a rhetorical question

....

b) a simple sentence

....

c) a simile

....

d) repetition

....

Extend

Write two or three paragraphs exploring the effect on the reader of the use of an intrusive narrator in *A Christmas Carol*.

Answers

Pages 4–5

Revise 1

a) Marley has died: 'Marley was dead'

b) They were business partners: 'Scrooge and he were partners'

c) He was unconcerned/uncaring: 'not so dreadfully cut up'

Revise 2

a) He is a bad employer – he will not let him have extra coal and resents him having a day off.

b) He is unfriendly/critical/ungrateful for the invitation.

c) He is rude and argumentative, refusing to give them money.

d) He is angry and frightens him off.

Revise 3

Answers might explore: the use of lists of adjectives; pathetic fallacy (the weather reflecting mood); the imagery of light and dark; the metaphor 'phantoms' foreshadowing the appearance of the ghosts; adjectives associated with dirt; the personification of nature; alliteration, e.g. 'bleak, biting'; similes, e.g. 'like ruddy smears …'.

Extend

Answers might include: the use of sound; the use of humour to convey Scrooge's scepticism and attempts to avoid the truth; the language of horror and fear in the description of Scrooge's reactions; the use of the conventions of the ghost story; the way in which the narrative both amuses and frightens readers.

Comic Strip

'Are there no prisons?'

Pages 6–7

Revise 1

a) Ghost of Christmas Past, **b)** Scrooge, **c)** Fan, **d)** Fred, **e)** Fezziwig, **f)** Belle

Revise 2

a) Scrooge was a lonely but imaginative child.

b) His father did not care for him.

c) He was cheerful and sociable as a young man. Mr Fezziwig shows it is possible to be a good employer, unlike Scrooge.

d) He has suffered because of his love of money.

Revise 3

a) Answers should include: the use of adjectives to convey the way the place is uncared for and cold, reflecting the young Scrooge's loneliness and the way he has been neglected by his family.

b) Answers should include: the use of parallel phrasing ('the floor was swept and watered, the lamps were trimmed …') to give a sense of activity and excitement; the emphasis on light and warmth, reflecting Fezziwig's character.

c) Answers should include: the contrast between the modesty of the room and its 'comfort', reflecting how Belle is happy despite not being rich.

Extend

Answers might explore: the strength of Scrooge's emotions, reflected in his language; the warmth and love shown between Belle and her family; how Scrooge imagines himself in the husband's place; how he hears his own loneliness casually referred to; the impact of seeing images of his past in the Ghost's face; how the Ghost's light disturbs him; the light as a symbol of knowledge and understanding.

Comic Strip

'A solitary child, neglected by his friends, is left there still.'

Pages 8–9

Revise 1

1. The Ghost of Christmas Present takes Scrooge through the streets of London.

2. Scrooge watches the Cratchits at Christmas dinner.

3. The Ghost takes Scrooge around the country, where he sees different people celebrating Christmas.

4. Scrooge enjoys watching Fred and his family celebrating Christmas.

5. The Ghost shows Ignorance and Want to Scrooge.

Revise 2

a) Bob does not judge or criticise Scrooge, calling him the 'Founder of the Feast', but his wife reacts angrily.

b) Fred's wife is critical of Scrooge and thinks him mean but Fred finds him amusing and pities him ('I feel sorry for him'), thinking he harms 'nobody but himself'.

Revise 3

Answers might include: the contrast between the cold outside and the warmth inside; descriptions of the wildness of nature, reflecting the harshness of life on the moors and at sea; the use of the language of violence to describe nature; the imagery of light and warmth indicating conviviality and togetherness, and used to describe the people celebrating Christmas; the references to religion and tradition.

Extend

Answers might include: the range of people from different places and social classes; the emphasis on family life; the depiction of both plenty and poverty; how he starts with general scenes of London at Christmas, demonstrating 'Christmas spirit', then the focus on the Cratchits making him think about his own life and his relationship to them; the series of small scenes giving a wider sense of life in Victorian Britain; Fred's party showing Scrooge what he is missing and how he is thought of; and finally the shock of seeing Ignorance and Want changing the mood and giving a warning both to Scrooge and the reader.

Comic Strip

'Mr Scrooge! I give you Mr Scrooge, the founder of the feast!'

Pages 10–11

Revise 1

a) = 4, **b)** = 5, **c)** = 2, **d)** = 1, **e)** = 3

Revise 2

a) Mrs Dilber – She believes he deserved to die alone.

b) Caroline's husband – He is glad that Scrooge is dead.

c) A 'man of business' – He is indifferent and makes a joke of Scrooge's death.

Revise 3

Answers might include: **Scrooge's deathbed** the use of contrasting imagery of light and darkness; use of a triplet ('unwatched, unwept, uncared for'); personification of Death and Dickens' direct address to it; the use of rhetorical questions and exclamations; the animals used to create an eerie atmosphere; **Tiny Tim's deathbed** the effect of the dialogue between the Cratchits; religious references; the positive sense created by the use of words such as 'pleasantly', 'cheerful' and 'happy' (perhaps unexpected in a deathbed scene).

Extend

Answers might include: the way in which Dickens avoids identifying the dead man as Scrooge; whether and when readers might realise it is Scrooge; the changes in mood from the light-hearted banter of the businessmen through the dark humour of the pawnshop to the horror of the bedroom; the effect of the revelation of the grave; the effect of the Ghost of Christmas Yet to Come's appearance and silence; Scrooge's sympathy for the dead man and his disgust at the scene in the pawnshop; what the events tell Scrooge about his reputation and his possible fate.

Comic Strip

'It would have done you good to see how green a place it is.'

Pages 12–13

Revise 1

a) Living in the Past means remembering and learning from past experiences.

b) Living in the Present means taking an interest, and participating, in the world.

c) Living in the Future means considering the results of his actions and trying to improve society.

Revise 2

a) He treated him meanly, not allowing him extra coal and not wanting to give him time off, but now he is generous.

b) He reacted angrily to his invitation and disapproved of his marriage, but now he wants to be part of his family and join in the fun at Christmas.

c) He argued with them and refused to donate, but now he makes an effort to give generously.

Revise 3

Answers might include: the use of direct speech as he talks to himself; the use of exclamations; the use of colloquial/slang terms such as 'Whoop'; the series of similes to describe his mood; short sentences and active verbs conveying activity; the repetition of words like 'chuckle' to emphasise his childlike happiness.

Extend

Answers might include: the contrast between his behaviour here and in Stave 1; the childlike enthusiasm shown in his speech; the sense of activity and energy; the use of the portly gentlemen to show how much he has changed; the similarities and differences between the two descriptions of Fred's Christmas; references to religion and Christian teaching; Dickens' role as an intrusive narrator; the description of the changed Scrooge at the end of the novel.

Comic Strip

'that he knew how to keep Christmas well.'

Pages 14–15

Revise 1

a) Exposition – introducing characters, settings, etc. at the beginning of a story.

b) Cliffhanger – an event at the end of a section of text (e.g. a chapter) that makes the reader want to know what happens next.

c) Flashback – part of the narrative that describes events that happened before the start of the main action (out of chronological order).

d) Circular structure – an ending that refers back to the beginning of the story so that the reader reflects on how things have changed.

Revise 2

a) Makes the reader wonder why it is important that Marley is dead and foreshadows the appearance of his ghost.

b) Shows how important family life is and celebrates childhood.

c) Tells readers that they too should behave like the reformed Scrooge.

Revise 3

Answers might include: the importance of the Christian message in the novel; the special 'spirit of Christmas'; carols being both spiritual and entertaining; the idea that the novel can be seen as a celebration of Christmas; the way the musical term 'staves' relates to the novel's title.

Extend

Answers might include: how each stave and the appearance of each Ghost represents a new stage in Scrooge's story; the extent to which he has changed at the end of each stave; ideas about psychological

development; ideas about spiritual development and redemption; the use of a circular structure as the end refers back to the beginning; the importance of the 'flashbacks' in Stave 2; the way in which characters such as the Cratchits and Fred recur at different points in the narrative; Dickens' intrusive narrative style.

Comic Strip

'God bless Us, Every One.'

Pages 16–17

Revise 1

a) True, **b)** False, **c)** True, **d)** True

Revise 2

a) He wanted to draw attention to the plight of the poor, especially poor children.

b) He thought that an entertaining story would reach more people and have more influence on attitudes.

Revise 3

Answers might focus on: the descriptions of the Cratchits being influenced by his own family's situation when he was a child; the descriptions of the pawnshop and the area it is in recalling the time his father was in prison; Belle's family being similar to his own large family; his love of Christmas parties and games; the depiction of Ignorance and Want being influenced by what he saw in London and his interest in social reform.

Extend

Answers might include: the way Marley is depicted as a 'traditional' ghost that readers might be used to reading about; Dickens' awareness that this is the case and his comments on it; the language of fear and horror; the build-up to Marley's Ghost; symbols of chains etc.; the extension of the idea of ghosts to include spirits that represent ideas rather than dead people; the supernatural abilities of the Ghosts, for example travelling through time and space; their association (especially the Ghost of Christmas Present) with religious ideas; the symbolism in the description of each Ghost.

Pages 18–19

Revise 1

b) and **d)**

Revise 2

a) Adjectives – gloomy, sooty, dingy

b) Personification – 'all the chimneys in Great Britain … were blazing away to their dear hearts' content.'

Revise 3

Answers might include: the long lists giving a sense of abundance; personification of foods such as onions and chestnuts to comic effect; the use of exclamation; the language of luxury and richness; the sense of excitement conveyed in the description of the people's actions; the symbolism of the Ghost's torch.

Extend

Possible choices include: Fred's house/the pawnshop; the description of the shops at Christmas/the description of Ignorance

and Want; Scrooge's house and office/the Cratchits' home. Answers could refer to: the contrast between plenty and poverty; the use of pathetic fallacy to associate places with characters; symbolism of light and dark; the use of personification.

Pages 20–21

Revise 1

a) The portly gentlemen, **b)** Mrs Fezziwig, **c)** Peter Cratchit, **d)** The sailors, **e)** Mrs Dilber

Revise 2

a) Married women were expected to work in the home and focus on their families (many women enjoyed this role of provider/nurturer).

b) Young women were judged by their looks and personalities and were concerned with romance and finding husbands.

c) A woman's future might depend on whether she could bring money to a marriage.

Revise 3

Answers might include: they are poor but not desperate – indicated by the gown being 'twice-turned' and Peter wearing his father's collar; the sense that they aspire to be respectable by being smartly dressed; the gentle humour at the expense of their aspirations.

Extend

You could choose any two characters from Fan, Belle, Mrs Cratchit, Martha Cratchit, Mrs Fezziwig, the charwoman, the laundress, Caroline, Fred's wife or Fred's sister-in-law. Contrasts could be based on their social position, their attitudes, their domestic roles, their appearance, their characters, what they do and say, Dickens' comments on them and other characters' reactions to them.

Pages 22–23

Revise 1

a) Answers might focus on comparison with characters who are wealthier and characters who are poorer than the Cratchits.

b) She is described as being 'dowerless' so does not have a lot of money. However, she is clearly middle class and not in dire need.

c) They are in low-paid casual work so earn very little. However, they make more money than most working-class people, but they make it dishonestly.

Revise 2

Quotations you might have chosen include:

a) 'Many can't go there; and many would rather die.'

b) 'Yellow, meagre, ragged, scowling, wolfish'

c) 'the people half naked, drunken, slipshod, ugly.'

Revise 3

Answers might include references to: Scrooge's lack of family and his need to be independent; the change in him between his time as an apprentice and when he breaks off the engagement to

Belle; his love of money shown then; his meanness; his solitariness; the way in which he lives despite being rich; his refusal to acknowledge any responsibility to others.

Extend

Answers might include: the gentlemen's action in collecting for charity; their association of charity with Christmas and Christianity; their concern about the workings of the Poor Law and their knowledge of its consequences; Scrooge's lack of compassion; his assertion that prisons and workhouses deal with the problem; his feeling that it is none of his business; his reference to overpopulation and his callousness about people dying; the use of dialogue to present arguments about poverty and inform the reader; Scrooge's abruptness; the contrast between his rudeness and the gentlemen's politeness.

Pages 24–25

Revise 1

a) Morality, b) Christmas Day, c) The New Testament, d) Sin, e) Compassion, f) The Ten Commandments

Revise 2

a) They are following Christian teaching by helping others.

b) He is showing generosity and forgiveness.

c) They are worshipping God.

Revise 3

Answers might refer to: adjectives often used in hymns and carols to describe Christ being used to describe Tiny Tim (e.g. 'patient', 'mild'); the repetition of 'little' before 'child' emphasising how young Tiny Tim was and perhaps associating his youth and innocence with the baby Jesus; the idea that quarrelling would dishonour Tim's memory and that such behaviour would also be against Christ's teachings.

Extend

Answers might include: Scrooge goes to church; he buys the turkey for the Cratchits and gives money to the portly gentlemen; he becomes reconciled with Fred; he is described as being almost childlike; his excitement about Christmas; his determination to change; the pleasant and affectionate way in which he addresses people.

Pages 26–27

Revise 1

a) Adjectives – tight-fisted, squeezing, wrenching, grasping, scraping, clutching, covetous

b) Simile – 'solitary as an oyster'

c) Metaphor – 'The cold within him'

d) Physical features – nose, cheek, gait, eyes, lips, voice

Revise 2

a) He is short-tempered and he hates Christmas.

b) He lacks compassion and he is argumentative.

c) He is solitary, sad and obsessed with money.

Revise 3

Answers might include: the use of pathetic fallacy, lists, anaphora and parallel phrasing; the impact of the repeated negative; personification of nature; use of a rhetorical question; use of the traditional fairy tale opening 'Once upon a time'.

Extend

Answers might include: the lack of comfort in Scrooge's home in contrast to his wealth; the transferred epithet of 'melancholy' reflecting Scrooge's mood and attitude; emphasis on Scrooge being alone; personification of the house; descriptions of the house ('old and gloomy') that could be applied to Scrooge himself; the mixture of horror and amusement in the description of Marley's face in the door knocker; Scrooge's initial fear and his defiant scepticism.

Comic Strip

'He carried his own low temperature always about with him.'

Pages 28–29

Revise 1

melancholy (used to describe the room but implies Scrooge's mood); a lonely boy; reading near a feeble fire; his poor forgotten self

Revise 2

Possible answers include:

a) '"But she had a large heart!"
"So she had," cried Scrooge.'
This shows Scrooge's appreciation of Fan's love.

b) 'The happiness he gives is quite as great as if it cost a fortune.'
Scrooge appreciates the effects of Fezziwig's generosity and good nature.

c) 'Why do you delight to torture me?'
Scrooge's emotional reaction shows how painful it is for him to remember his mistakes.

Revise 3

Answers might include: references to Scrooge's loneliness as a boy; how he finds escape in reading as a boy, in contrast to his lack of interest in anything except money as an adult; his reaction to Fan in contrast to his reaction to Fred; the contrast between his enforced solitariness as a child and his choice to be alone as an adult; his reaction to seeing himself as a boy; the effect of the section on the reader's perception of Scrooge, as he becomes a more sympathetic character.

Extend

Answers might include: how, by this point, Scrooge has learned from the past, the present and the future; his emotional reaction both to seeing himself and seeing how others live; his shock at the circumstances of his own 'death'; the pathetic fallacy of the description of the graveyard; the use of images associated with horror and the supernatural; Scrooge's questioning of the Ghost followed by an emotional reaction when he sees his name; the use of direct speech to convey Scrooge's desire to change; the spirit's reaction.

Comic Strip

'I will honour Christmas in my heart and try to keep it all the year.'

Pages 30–31

Revise 1

Possible answers include:

a) 'the spirit raised a frightful cry'

b) 'Or would you know,' pursued the Ghost, 'the weight and length of the strong coil you bear yourself?'

c) 'No rest. No peace. Incessant torture of remorse.'

Revise 2

a) It is there to bring Scrooge knowledge/illumination.

b) It intends to redeem/save Scrooge.

c) It is determined to make Scrooge confront his past.

d) It cannot be resisted.

Revise 3

Answers might refer to: the use of dialogue; humour; the symbolism of Marley's chain; the stress laid on his similarity to Scrooge; the horror of what he has become; the use of religious language and references such as 'penance'.

Extend

Answers might include: the need for Scrooge to relive his past; the effect of this on him and the reader; the strange appearance of the Ghost (like an old man and a child, symbolic references to winter/summer); the significance of the light coming from its head; its gentle manner contrasting with its firmness; Scrooge's attempts to resist the Ghost; what the Ghost helps Scrooge to learn about himself; the way Dickens uses the genre of the ghost story; the way it helps to explore Scrooge's psychological development.

Comic Strip

'No. Your past.'

Pages 32–33

Revise 1

shrouded, black, night, darkness

Revise 2

a) The torch is symbolic of the spirit of Christmas and is later used by the Ghost to spread that spirit.

b) It refers to a Christmas tradition which originated in the pagan winter solstice.

c) It shows that enjoyment, hospitality and generosity are important parts of Christmas and implies how people should behave, especially at Christmas.

d) It shows that Christmas is a time of peace.

Revise 3

Answers might refer to: not seeing the Ghost's face adds to the mystery and fear; the association of the Ghost with depictions of death; the need for Scrooge to work things out for himself; the effect on the reader of not having things explained by the Ghost.

Extend

Answers might include: associations with Christmas traditions; the physical appearance of the Ghost; its association with plenty; the significance of its torch; the idea of the Spirit of Christmas; the importance of Scrooge seeing how others celebrate Christmas and how they live; its role in exposing social problems through Ignorance and Want; how the things it shows Scrooge change him.

Comic strip

'a jolly Giant, glorious to see.'

Pages 34–35

Revise 1

a) Tiny Tim, b) Martha, c) Peter, d) Mrs Cratchit

Revise 2

Answers might include: the contrast between the misery inside the office and his happiness when he gets outside; his association with children and simple pleasures; the reference to him as 'the clerk' rather than by his name; the colloquial noun 'twinkling' suggesting quickness and magic; his lack of money shown by having 'no great coat'; the sense of enthusiasm and joy conveyed by the active verbs 'ran', 'pelt' and 'play'.

Revise 3

Answers might include: the warmth with which he is referred to; the physical and verbal affection shown to him by the children; the care he takes of Tiny Tim; his praise for his wife; his attitude to the death of Tiny Tim.

Extend

Answers might include: the significance of Tiny Tim's handicap; Dickens' deliberate lack of precision about its nature and possible causes; his cheerfulness; his acceptance of his condition; Bob's attachment to and care for him; his position in the family; his references to religion; his association with Jesus; his enjoyment of Christmas despite his suffering; contrast between him and Scrooge as a boy; the pathos of his 'death'; the way in which his plight moves Scrooge; Scrooge's anxiety about his fate; how Scrooge acts toward him at the end of the novel ('a second father').

Comic Strip

'My dear, the children! Christmas day!'

Pages 36–37

Revise 1

a) generous, energetic, warm, playful
b) delicate, loving, optimistic, eager

Revise 2

a) Unlike Scrooge, Fan is affectionate and warm. He is cold and lacking emotion.
b) Unlike Fred, Scrooge is bad-tempered. Fred is much more friendly, especially towards Bob.

Revise 3

Answers might include: the impact of opening with 'merry Christmas', demonstrating the contrast with Scrooge; his use of the title 'uncle'; the use of exclamation; the speed of his entrance and the references to activity; Scrooge's unfriendly reaction; the warmth emphasised in the description of Fred contrasted with the cold in previous descriptions of Scrooge;

the impression given of good health; the positive description of his ruddy and 'handsome' looks.

Extend

Answers might include: the importance of them being mother and son; Fan being shown as a child with implications of innocence; Fan used to show that Scrooge was once loved; the revelation of the problems with his father; Fan's positive attitude and optimism; ways in which Fred is similar to Fan; Fred's celebration of Christmas in contrast to Scrooge's; Fred's home as an example of a happy Victorian family; his sense of fun and lack of bitterness; the way in which the Ghost uses Fan to remind Scrooge of Fred; Scrooge rediscovering his love for Fan; Scrooge's unexpected enjoyment of Fred's party; the contrast between Fan's delicate nature and Fred's robustness; the positive language used by both of them and about both of them.

Comic strip

'Because I fell in love.'

Pages 38–39

Revise 1

a) He is happy and successful.
b) He is energetic and enthusiastic.
c) He is part of a close couple. He is hospitable, polite and caring.

Revise 2

a) eager, greedy, restless
b) In a mourning dress
c) tears

Revise 3

Answers might refer to Scrooge's status as an apprentice and Bob's as a clerk; the young Scrooge's enjoyment of his work; Fezziwig's personality in contrast with his own; Fezziwig's generosity to his employees contrasted with Scrooge's meanness to Bob; Fezziwig's celebration of Christmas contrasting with Scrooge's resentment of Bob having a day off.

Extend

Answers might include: Dickens as an intrusive narrator; his seeing the scene from a child's point of view; the contrast of the large happy family with Scrooge's solitary life; the description of Belle as a contented 'matron'; the modest but comfortable home; the use of war-like imagery to convey the happy chaos of the family; the relationship between Belle and her husband; the importance of children at Christmas; Scrooge's admiration of Belle and his jealousy; how the scene causes him to regret his past and see how his life might have been if he had not loved money so much; the emotional pain it causes him shown in what he says to the Ghost.

Comic Strip

'… is quite as great as if it cost a fortune.'

Pages 40–41

Revise 1

a) True, b) False, c) True, d) True, e) False, f) True

Revise 2

a) He wonders why the torch makes people happy and stops quarrels.
b) 'There is. My own.'
c) The Ghost represents the spirit of Christmas and this spirit is symbolised in the incense he spreads, changing people's behaviour.

Revise 3

Answers might include: Fred's use of religious language ('veneration' and 'sacred'); Dickens' use of dashes to create an aside where he reminds readers of the religious meaning of Christmas; the long sentence giving an impression of his enthusiasm and sincerity; the list of positive adjectives to define the 'time'; the metaphor of people opening up their hearts; his use of contrasting similes to give an idea of how Christmas reminds us of how to behave towards others.

Extend

Answers might include: the men collecting for charity; the busy street scene showing people enjoying themselves; Fred's generosity and hospitality; the behaviour of the Cratchits; the differing celebrations of Christmas that Scrooge is shown across the country; the emphasis on kindness; the part played by traditions; the emphasis on enjoyment; the significance of the Ghost's torch; the contrast with Scrooge's attitude; the idea that the spirit of Christmas should last throughout the year; the importance of remembering that Christmas is a religious festival.

Comic strip

'he shed a few drops of water on them from it, and their good-humour was restored directly.'

Pages 42–43

Revise 1

a) miser b) marry c) charity d) greed e) loves f) earn g) dishonestly h) consequences

Revise 2

a) a monstrous iron safe, b) piteously, c) wretched

Revise 3

Answers might include: the use of the simple sentence at the start to convey the strength of Scrooge's feeling; the emotive noun 'horror'; the darkness of the scene; the alliteration of the nouns 'detestation' and 'disgust' to convey his reaction; the comparison of the people to demons, expressing their immorality; the use of the horrific idea of selling a body; the reader's awareness that the characters' love of money is similar to Scrooge's.

Extend

Answers might include: the stark contrast between this scene and the previous one at the Fezziwigs' party; how the physical description of Scrooge reflects his character; the dialogue in which Belle confronts him with the change in his character; the powerful symbol of the golden idol; her characterisation of 'Gain' as the 'master passion'; the reader's awareness of this being a turning point in Scrooge's life; the importance of marriage to Belle and her strength in rejecting a rich husband; the strength of Scrooge's emotional reaction, including his use of the metaphor 'torture'.

Comic strip

'A golden one.'

Pages 44–45

Revise 1

a) lack of knowledge and/or education

b) poverty – the lack of food and money

Revise 2

a) Children are particularly at risk from poverty and depicting Ignorance and Want as children would evoke more sympathy as they are thought of as innocent victims.

b) It emphasises that they are serious problems at the time of writing/reading.

c) People are responsible for poverty and ignorance.

d) If nothing is done about ignorance, society will be destroyed.

Revise 3

Answers might include: the reference to an ideal of childhood and its contrast with Ignorance and Want; personification of 'graceful youth' and 'shrivelled hand'; the use of violent verbs ('pinched', 'twisted' and 'pulled'); the antithesis of angels and devils; the sense of danger and threat conveyed by 'menacing'.

Extend

Answers might include: Dickens' motivation for writing the novel; his concern with child poverty; current ideas about the causes and effects of poverty and lack of education; the idea that Scrooge and the reader should take responsibility for social problems; the horrific imagery used to describe them; the significance of their being presented as children; Scrooge's reaction to seeing the children and his attempts to understand; the significance of 'Doom'; the shock created by the sudden appearance of them after scenes of plenty and enjoyment; the significance of the moment in Scrooge's redemption.

Comic strip

'on his brow I see that written which is Doom.'

Pages 46–47

Revise 1

a) = 3, b) = 4, c) = 6, d) = 2, e) = 1, f) = 5

Revise 2

a) 'the master of the house'

b) 'his daughter … her mother'

c) 'fondly'

d) 'at his own fireside'

Revise 3

Answers might include: the presentation of Scrooge's father as having been a stereotypical strict Victorian father; Fan's delight in the change; her comparison of their home to Heaven, implying joy and peace; her implication in 'I was not afraid' that the children might usually have been afraid of their father; the reader's growing awareness that Scrooge has been neglected for a long time; the assumption that a good family life will bring happiness.

Extend

Answers might focus on Scrooge's own family, Fred's family, Belle's family, the Cratchits, Caroline's family or the miner's family. Ideas for comparison might include: closeness and love contrasted with coldness and neglect; the make-up of each family; the social status and relative wealth/poverty of the families; the way the families celebrate Christmas; the language Dickens uses to describe their family life; his comments as narrator on family life; Scrooge's reactions to seeing the different families; how the range of families reflects the way different people lived in the 19th century; the importance of family life in Victorian society.

Comic strip

'and another generation beyond that.'

Pages 48–49

Revise 1

a) = 3, b) = 1, c) = 2

Revise 2

Answers might refer to: Dickens' use of direct address; the personification of death; the language of horror; the exclamation; the use of imperatives; the characterisation of someone who does not need to fear death; the confident tone; the use of 'thine/thy', which echoes the language of sermons and religious texts; the implied association with Christian morality.

Revise 3

Answers could include: surprise at the introduction of happiness and cheer; reaction to imagery of light; the sense that the dead Tim has not been left alone; a sense that this is seen as a good way to react after a death; the understated conveyance of Bob's sadness; reactions to Bob kissing Tim's face; the sense of pathos; whether a modern reader might consider this over-sentimental.

Extend

Answers might include: the light-hearted reaction of some to Scrooge's death; the feeling that no-one had cared for him in life; the only emotion felt in response to his death being happiness; the contrasting deep feeling at Tim's death; the lack of mourners for Scrooge; the empty room contrasted with the Cratchits' busy house; the contrasting imagery of dark and light; the sense of horror at Scrooge's death compared with the peacefulness of Tim's; the contrast between the graveyards; implied ideas of life after death; a sense that goodness lives on after death.

Comic strip

'Spirit of Tiny Tim, thy childish essence was from God!'

Pages 50–51

Revise 1

Possible answers include:

a) 'At this festive season of the year … it is more than usually desirable that we should make some slight provision for the poor and destitute'

b) 'I help to support the establishments I have mentioned'

c) 'It's not my business.'

Revise 2

a) He has preferred money to love and friendship and has rejected his family.

b) He does not pay Bob Cratchit well.

c) As a member of society and a voter, he is responsible for what happens to others.

Revise 3

Answers might include: Marley is responding to Scrooge's praise of him as a man of business; the double meaning of 'business'; the implication that Marley's actions affected others; the idea that had he understood what his business really was he would have acted differently; the implication that the virtues he mentions should be everyone's business.

Extend

Answers might include: the use of Ignorance and Want to make Scrooge aware of his responsibilities; the idea that all people are responsible for their existence; the idea that they are not natural but man-made; the implication that something can be done about them; the strength of the imagery and language used; the significance of 'Doom' on Ignorance's forehead; the extent of child poverty in Victorian England; the lack of education for the poor; the shock of their appearance.

Comic strip

'Who suffers by his ill whims? Himself always.'

Pages 52–53

Revise 1

1. Scrooge relives his past and starts to understand what he has done wrong.

2. Scrooge is shown what will happen if he does not reform and he decides to change.

3. Scrooge is redeemed and is a changed man.

Revise 2

a) penance, b) chance and hope, c) no light part

Revise 3

Answers might include: Scrooge's happiness and excitement; his child-like behaviour (as if born again); his generosity to the Cratchits; his donation to the portly gentlemen and the way this reminds us of his behaviour in Stave 1; the contrast between his attitude to the boy and his behaviour to the carol singer; his attendance at church; the way Dickens describes his changed personality at the end of the stave.

Extend

Answers might include: consideration of the meaning of the word; its Christian context; the importance of the story being set at Christmas; the stages of Scrooge's redemption represented by the Ghosts; the importance of him atoning for his past actions; the symbolism of his 'death' in Stave 4, suggesting he must be re-born; the role played by Tiny Tim in Scrooge's

Grade	AO1 (12 marks)	AO2 (12 marks)	AO3 (6 marks)
6–7+ (17–30 marks)	A convincing, well-structured essay that answers the question fully. Quotations and references are well-chosen and integrated into sentences. The response covers the whole novel.	Analysis of the full range of Dickens' methods. Thorough exploration of the effects of these methods. Accurate range of subject terminology.	Exploration is linked to specific aspects of the novel's contexts to show a detailed understanding.
4–5 (11–16 marks)	A clear essay that always focuses on the exam question. Quotations and references support ideas effectively. The response refers to different points in the novel.	Explanation of Dickens' different methods. Clear understanding of the effects of these methods. Accurate use of subject terminology.	References to relevant aspects of context show a clear understanding.
2–3 (5–10 marks)	The essay has some good ideas that are mostly relevant. Some quotations and references are used to support the ideas.	Identification of some different methods used by Dickens to convey meaning. Some subject terminology.	Some awareness of how ideas in the novel link to its context.

redemption; the idea that those who are willing to change can be redeemed.

Comic strip

'I am not the man I was.'

Pages 54–71

Exam Practice

Use the mark scheme above to self-assess your strengths and weaknesses. Work up from the bottom, putting a tick by things you have fully accomplished, a ½ by skills that are in place but need securing, and underlining areas that need particular development. The estimated grade boundaries are included so you can assess your progress towards your target grade.

Pages 54–56

Answers might include: Fred's cheerful, outgoing personality in contrast to Scrooge; Fred's reaching out to Scrooge as a family member; his enjoyment of Christmas; his celebration of Christmas with his family; his choice of love over money, shown by his marriage (in contrast to Scrooge's broken engagement); his understanding of the spirit of Christmas; his direct link of the celebration with its religious meaning; the hospitality he shows others; the warmth and comfort of his home, in contrast to Scrooge's rooms; his child-like playfulness; his link to Fan and similarities to her; the way the Cratchits talk about him in Stave 4.

Pages 57–59

Answers might include: the physical description of Scrooge reflecting the psychological changes in him; the symbolism of the 'growing tree'; the symbolism of the golden idol; the contrast between Belle's gentleness and Scrooge's impatience; their contrasting reactions to the idea of being poor; her confrontation of him with how he has changed and his defence that he is no longer a boy; the contrast between Scrooge here and Scrooge at the Fezziwigs' party; the way in which the Ghost has guided him through his past and helped him and the reader to understand how and why he has changed; how the visits of the Ghosts enable him to change again.

Pages 60–62

Answers might include: the contrast of the harsh environment with the homely scene; the focus on family life; people enjoying themselves despite poverty; the

way in which Christmas transforms the old man; tradition in the singing of Christmas songs; the symbolism of light; contrast between the lives of the miners and the lighthouse keepers but similarity in their celebrating of Christmas; the link between the celebrations and the religious meaning of Christmas; the Ghost of Christmas Present as a symbolic figure; the use of the Ghost's torch to spread the spirit of Christmas; how Christmas is honoured by helping others and showing love and kindness to family and to strangers.

Pages 63–65

Answers might include: the family united in grief; Bob's innocent and amusing reaction to Fred's polite enquiries; Bob's love and respect for his wife, echoed by the children; the way in which they look forward optimistically to the future; their determination to remember Tim; their affectionate physical contact; the writer's direct address to Tiny Tim; his association with God; their social status and relative poverty; their hard work; the difference between Mr and Mrs Cratchit's attitudes to Scrooge; their enjoyment of their modest Christmas; their role in changing Scrooge.

Pages 66–68

Answers might include: Scrooge's joy at waking up on Christmas morning; his activity and energy; his child-like pleasure in life; the use of exclamations and colloquialisms; his bringing together of Past, Present and Future, showing that he has learned from all three Ghosts; emotion shown in his tears; reference back to the pawnshop; the use of similes to express his changed personality; the contrast between the Scrooge described here and the Scrooge of Stave 1; his recollection of some previous incidents; his growing awareness in previous staves of his failings and the need to change; his initial resistance shown in his attempt to extinguish the Ghost of Christmas Past's light; the impact of seeing his own death; his subsequent actions in Stave 5 showing how much he has changed.

Pages 69–71

Answers might include: the double meaning of 'business'; the introduction of the religious concept of 'penance'; the mixture of humour and horror in the portrayal of Marley's Ghost; the idea that

Marley is paying for his sins after death, with connotations of heaven and hell; the symbolism of the chain; the message that Marley's and Scrooge's avarice is sinful; the overt references to the birth of Christ giving a religious context; Marley's role in Scrooge's redemption; the idea that Scrooge and the reader are responsible for the suffering of others; references to Christ being born to redeem mankind; the stages Scrooge goes through to be redeemed; the final stave's message that redemption is possible and brings happiness.

Pages 72–73

Revise 1

a) = 4, b) = 2, c) = 5, d) = 1, e) = 3

Revise 2

a) Simile, b) Metaphor, c) Personification, d) Pathetic fallacy

Revise 3

a) Scrooge: he is the main character/it is his story.

b) An intrusive narrator: he interrupts the action to speak to the reader.

c) Stave 1: Dickens sets the scene, introduces Scrooge and gives some background to the story.

Revise 4

Answers might include:

a) 'Scrooge knew he was dead?' 'How could it be otherwise?'

b) 'Scrooge signed it.' 'Old Marley was as dead as a door nail.'

c) 'dead as a door nail'

d) 'His sole executor, his sole administrator, his sole assign, his sole residuary legatee, his sole friend, and sole mourner.'

Extend

Answers might include: the establishment of a friendly tone; an insight into the author's views; a sense of involvement in the story, helping to make the readers care about it; the way in which Dickens can appeal directly to the reader; the introduction of humour to the narrative.

Snap up other workbooks from Collins:

9780008355265

9780008355272

9780008355289

9780008355296

9780008355302

9780008355319

9780008355326

9780008355333

Browse online at
collins.co.uk/revision